YOUTUBE HACKS

YOUTUBE HACKS

Secrets to Boost Your Views and Engagement

B. VINCENT

RWG Publishing

CONTENTS

CHAPTER 1

The Anatomy of a Viral Video: What Makes Content Stick?

Viral videos in the internet ecosystem spread rapidly, generating buzz, shares, and discussions. They can be compared to spontaneous wildfires. Many individuals have encountered a viral video and have pondered the reasons behind its widespread popularity. Many creators are interested in understanding how to intentionally create such a phenomenon. This analysis aims to explore the structural components of a viral video and identify the factors that contribute to its lasting impact.

Emotional resonance is a key factor in the virality of content. Videos that elicit intense emotional responses, such as amusement, sadness, anger, or motivation, are more prone to being shared. When individuals establish an emotional connection with a particular piece of content, their act of sharing extends beyond the video itself; it encompasses the sentiment it evokes within them. Reflecting on the most impactful viral videos one has encountered, they have the ability to evoke strong emotional responses, such as laughter, tears, or a profound sense of connection to a particular cause.

Relatability is a fundamental aspect of human nature, as individuals tend to identify with and find connections in stories and narratives. When a video portrays a universally relatable experience or emotion, it fosters a sense of personal connection among viewers. The artwork may present a straightforward representation of everyday challenges or offer a lighthearted perspective on prevalent social observations. When content is relatable, individuals tend to share it among their social network, expressing sentiments such as "This resonates with me!" or "We can all relate to this experience!"

Simplicity and clarity are key factors in viral videos, as they tend to have a singular and easily understandable message or theme. The simplicity of the video prevents potential distractions from overshadowing its main message. In an era characterized by diminishing attention spans, the importance of clarity cannot be overstated.

Not all viral videos are filmed using high-end equipment, but they can still have high-quality production. The production quality should align with the video's content and purpose. High-quality audio and video are crucial for comedic sketches and informational content. The unedited quality of a spontaneous video clip can enhance its appeal. Always ensure that the content is both audible and visually engaging.

Shareability encompasses the aforementioned points. Videos that possess emotional resonance, relatability, and clarity tend to have a higher propensity for being shared. Additional factors that can enhance shareability include an attention-grabbing title, visually appealing thumbnail, or a compelling opening scene. Videos that have a compelling introduction within the initial seconds are more likely to maintain the attention of viewers.

The internet is saturated with content. Originality is distinctive. An original perspective, a new concept, or a creative delivery can attract attention and encourage sharing. Numerous viral videos have presented novel concepts or unexpected elements that were previously unseen.

Leveraging contemporary events, trends, or cultural changes can greatly enhance the likelihood of a video achieving viral status. The purpose is not to exploit opportunities, but to place content within the context of ongoing discussions. By engaging in this practice, you are able to leverage the pre-existing enthusiasm and momentum surrounding a particular subject.

Engaging content frequently elicits discussion, debate, or interaction. User engagement plays a crucial role in enhancing the visibility of videos on platforms such as YouTube. Algorithms prioritize content that receives comments, arguments, and discussions from viewers, thereby increasing its exposure.

Surprise can be a potent tool. The inclusion of unpredictability in a video, such as unexpected twists, emotional depth, or narrative shifts, can enhance its memorability for viewers.

Content that is accessible and inclusive has a greater likelihood of going viral, as it appeals to a wide audience and can transcend cultural barriers. Subtitles have the potential to enhance accessibility for individuals who are non-native speakers or have hearing impairments. Inclusivity aims to prevent any form of exclusion among different groups.

In conclusion, although the phenomenon of virality may appear arbitrary or coincidental, there is a discernible pattern or strategy behind it. The aforementioned elements serve as a guide for creators seeking to captivate the internet's collective imagination. Authenticity and passion are crucial when engaging in content creation. Although achieving virality is desirable, it should not overshadow the primary objective of creating meaningful and impactful content.

CHAPTER 2

Thumbnail Mastery: Creating Click-worthy First Impressions

On YouTube, the thumbnail of a video serves as its storefront window in the busy digital marketplace, enticing potential viewers to explore further. Similar to how an attractive window display can attract customers to a store, a carefully crafted thumbnail can greatly enhance click-through rates and subsequently, viewership. How can one ensure that their thumbnail stands out among a large amount of content? This article provides a comprehensive examination of techniques for mastering the skill of creating thumbnails.

Familiarize yourself with the guidelines of the platform. Prior to delving into design principles, it is advisable to acquaint oneself with the specifications for YouTube thumbnails. Based on the most recent training data from September 2021, it is advised to use an image size of 1280x720 pixels, with a minimum width of 640 pixels. Thumbnails should adhere to a 16:9 aspect ratio and have a file size below 2MB.

Begin with a high-resolution image to ensure optimal image quality. Unclear or low-resolution thumbnails can create an unprofessional appearance and discourage potential viewers. To ensure optimal image quality, it is important to capture a sharp and clear image, whether it is extracted from a video or obtained separately.

Humans are naturally attracted to faces. Thumbnails featuring emotive facial expressions, such as laughter, tears, or surprise, tend to attract higher click rates. Close-ups or medium shots that prominently display the face are most effective.

Utilize contrast to enhance the visibility and prominence of elements. Adjusting the brightness and contrast can enhance the visual appeal of a thumbnail, particularly when it is displayed on smaller screens such as mobile phones. However, it is important to avoid excessive alterations that result in an artificial appearance of the image.

Clear and Legible Text: When incorporating text in a thumbnail, it is important to ensure that the text is easily readable, succinct, and sufficiently sized for comfortable viewing. Choose bold, sans-serif typefaces and ensure a noticeable contrast between the text and its background. It is important to be discerning when choosing text for your thumbnail. Avoid clutter and excessive wording that may make it difficult to read or resemble a complete sentence.

Maintaining brand consistency in thumbnails can enhance brand recall for regular content creators and brands. Consistent visual elements such as color schemes, font types, and logo placement can enhance brand recognition among subscribers.

Utilize contextual imagery that offers a subtle indication of the video's subject matter. Misleading thumbnails can attract initial clicks, but if the content does not align with viewers' expectations, they are likely to disengage, potentially impacting the video's ranking in YouTube's algorithm.

Experiment and Adjust: Do not hesitate to modify your thumbnail if you perceive that it is not achieving the intended click-through rate. YouTube Studio offers analytics that can provide insights into the performance of your thumbnail. Based on these insights, one can engage in experimentation and adaptation.

When creating a thumbnail for YouTube, it is important to consider mobile users as a significant portion of the platform's viewership comes from mobile devices. Therefore, the thumbnail should be designed to be effective and visually appealing at both large and small sizes. Before finalizing, it is recommended to zoom out or view the thumbnail on a mobile screen to ensure that all elements remain clear and impactful.

Avoid using clickbait techniques. Using exaggerated images or claims in thumbnails to increase click rates may seem appealing, but this approach can have negative consequences. Clickbait can lead to viewer dissatisfaction and negatively impact a channel's long-term reputation. Strive for captivating content without being deceptive.

Utilize Thumbnail Tools: Numerous online tools, both free and paid, are accessible to aid in the creation of captivating thumbnails. Canva, Adobe Spark, and Fotor offer user-friendly design interfaces and pre-made templates specifically designed for YouTube thumbnails.

This study aims to analyze popular thumbnails. Each specific field has its own set of trends. Analyze thumbnails of popular videos within your category to identify recurring patterns or elements that appear to engage viewers. Although it is important not to plagiarize, seeking inspiration and studying successful examples can be advantageous.

Colors can elicit distinct emotions or reactions. Vibrant hues such as red, orange, and yellow possess the ability to swiftly attract attention; however, their usage should be exercised with discretion. Gain a comprehensive understanding of the psychological effects of colors and employ them strategically to subtly communicate the desired mood or theme of your video.

The best practices for thumbnails in digital marketing are subject to constant evolution. Keep yourself informed about YouTube's guidelines, design trends, and audience preferences. The effectiveness of certain strategies or approaches may require adjustment in the future.

In summary, a thumbnail serves a purpose beyond being a mere preview image for a video. Video optimization is a potent marketing tool that can greatly enhance the visibility and interaction of your videos. In the vast digital landscape, attention to small details can distinguish one from the rest. Investing time in mastering the skill of creating thumbnails can lead to significant returns.

CHAPTER 3

Crafting Captivating Titles: The Art and Science

The title of a YouTube video functions as an introductory element and an invitation to viewers. The thumbnail is the initial visual element that a prospective viewer encounters, and it plays a crucial role in influencing their decision to either click on the content or disregard it. Crafting an engaging title involves more than just being creative; it requires a combination of artistic and scientific elements. This analysis delves into the art of creating effective titles to optimize the reach and impact of your videos.

The Importance of Conciseness in Communication. It is crucial to maintain conciseness in YouTube titles as they are typically truncated after approximately 60 characters on most devices. To maximize visibility, it is advisable to position crucial information, such as keywords or the main topic, at the beginning of the text.

Highlight the significance or worth of something. The primary concern of a viewer is their personal benefit or gain. Make sure your title effectively communicates the value or benefit that readers will gain from the content. For instance, rather than using the title "My Trip to Hawaii," a more concise and academic alternative could be "Hawaii Travel Guide: Top 5 Must-Visit Spots!"

SEO, or Search Engine Optimization, is crucial in the field of science. Conduct a thorough keyword research to identify popular and relevant terms related to the subject matter of your video, and seamlessly integrate them into the title. Google's Keyword Planner and TubeBuddy are useful tools for this purpose.

Always avoid clickbait. Although sensational titles may initially attract clicks, they often result in rapid disengagement if the content fails to meet the viewer's expectations. This has the potential to negatively impact the algorithmic ranking of your video and undermine the credibility of your channel.

Utilizing interrogative titles can generate curiosity. Examples such as "How Does Photosynthesis Work?" or "Why is the Sky Blue?" pertain to specific inquiries that users may enter into search engines.

Numbers have an inherent appeal. Titles such as "10 Quick Breakfast Recipes" or "5 Tips for Enhancing Sleep Quality" are succinct and straightforward, offering a well-organized video content.

Emotional appeal can enhance the impact of a title. Descriptive terms such as "unbelievable," "heartwarming," or "hilarious" can provide viewers with a glimpse of the video's tone and attract their attention.

It is essential to ensure that the title of your video accurately represents its content. Misleading viewers can result in increased bounce rates, which can gradually erode the reputation of your channel.

Capitalization plays a significant role in communication. Although using ALL CAPS may initially appear attention-grabbing, it can be perceived as aggressive. Please utilize Title Case, which involves capitalizing the initial letter of significant words, in order to maintain a professional and easily readable format.

Testing and Iteration: Similar to thumbnails, it is advisable to modify the video title if it is not generating the desired response. It is advisable to regularly monitor your analytics in order to assess the impact of title changes on views and engagement.

Consider Your Audience: Customize your title to suit the specific audience you are addressing. For videos that explore intricate topics in depth, it is advisable to use a title that is more elaborate and precise. On the other hand, when targeting a wider range of individuals, it is advisable to present the information in a straightforward and easily understandable manner.

Incorporating elements of pop culture, trending topics, or current events can enhance the timeliness and relevance of your video.

Minimize the use of adjectives. Although descriptors can enhance the appeal of a title, excessive use of adjectives can create a contrived or insincere impression. Select one or two options that most effectively encapsulate the core message of your video.

Collaborations and Features: Incorporate the name of a renowned individual or brand in the title when engaging in a collaborative effort. It has the potential to attract a larger audience to your content.

Indicate the inclusion of a series in the title if your video is part of one. This phenomenon may promote excessive and prolonged viewing of content. An example is the title "Digital Marketing 101: Episode 3 – Social Media Strategies."

In conclusion, an engaging title serves as a potent asset in the realm of content marketing, surpassing its mere function as a descriptive label. By combining persuasive writing techniques with the principles of search engine optimization (SEO) and viewer psychology, it is possible to create titles that effectively attract and maintain viewer engagement. In the realm of YouTube, the title holds significant importance as it serves as the initial and sometimes sole opportunity to create an impact. Ensure that it is meaningful and significant.

CHAPTER 4

SEO for YouTube: Getting Your Videos to the Top

In the context of YouTube, the creation of exceptional content represents only a portion of the overall challenge. The remaining portion entails ensuring discoverability and viewership among the intended audience. SEO is crucial in this context. YouTube SEO involves optimizing different aspects of your video and channel to enhance its discoverability on the platform. Now, let us analyze the fundamental strategies that can effectively boost the visibility and ranking of your videos.

Keyword research is crucial. Prior to uploading, it is advisable to conduct thorough keyword research that is pertinent to your video. Tools such as YouTube's search suggest feature, Google's Keyword Planner, and specialized platforms like TubeBuddy or vidIQ can be utilized to identify search terms with high search volumes. Please include these elements in your title, description, and tags.

Optimize video titles by ensuring they are both captivating and contain relevant keywords. It is preferable to position the primary keyword at the start of the title. Please limit the text to a maximum of 60 characters for optimal visibility.

Provide Elaborate Descriptions: The video description allows for a substantial amount of text (up to 5,000 characters) to include relevant keywords and provide contextual information. The video provides a summary of its content, followed by a detailed breakdown, related content links, and a call to action for subscribing. The integration of keywords should be seamless and organic within the text.

Utilize Video Tags: Incorporate keyword phrases that may not be suitable for inclusion in the title or description. Annotations assist in providing contextual information to YouTube's algorithm regarding the content of your video. Utilize a combination of general and specific tags, ensuring their relevance at all times.

Custom thumbnails can enhance click-through rates, although they do not directly impact SEO. A higher click-through rate (CTR) has an indirect positive impact on search engine optimization (SEO) because it signals to YouTube that the video is more relevant to users.

Emphasize Video Quality: Videos with higher resolutions, such as 1080p or 4K, generally receive higher rankings compared to those with lower resolutions. Although content is important, the quality of the content is also significant.

Encouraging engagement through videos can positively impact their visibility on YouTube's algorithm, as increased likes, comments, shares, and subscribes are considered favorable. Promote audience engagement by posing inquiries and fostering discussions within the comment section.

Increasing watch time and retention is crucial for improving the ranking of your video. The higher the percentage and total duration of time that viewers spend watching your video, the more favorably it is ranked. Produce captivating content that effectively retains viewers' attention until the conclusion, while refraining from utilizing clickbait tactics that may result in rapid disengagement.

Creating playlists by grouping related videos together can enhance session watch time. Viewers watching multiple videos consecutively indicates to YouTube the value of your content.

Closed Captions (CC) and subtitles enhance video accessibility and contribute to improved search engine optimization (SEO) by providing additional text data for indexing on YouTube.

Sharing videos on various social media platforms, blogs, and websites can increase external traffic. Diversifying the audience and generating positive signals regarding the video's popularity are achieved through this approach.

Consistency and regularity in posting content are positively associated with improved search engine optimization (SEO) for channels. Engaging subscribers and demonstrating the channel's activity and value are both important aspects.

Optimize Channel Overall: Ensure that your channel is fully optimized for search engine optimization (SEO). The essential components for an effective channel are a description with relevant keywords, an engaging banner, and links to other social platforms or websites.

Collaborations can expand the reach of your content by introducing it to a new audience. Mutual promotion of videos by both parties can result in higher viewership, increased number of subscribers, and enhanced engagement.

YouTube's algorithm is constantly changing, so it is important to stay updated. To maintain the effectiveness of your SEO strategies, it is crucial to stay updated on the latest trends, changes, and best practices.

In conclusion, the creation of engaging content is crucial for the success of a YouTube channel. However, the implementation of SEO techniques is essential for optimizing this content and standing out in a highly competitive platform. By implementing video optimization techniques and gaining a comprehensive understanding of YouTube's search algorithm, content creators can enhance the visibility of their videos, thereby ensuring that their content reaches its intended audience. YouTube serves as both a social platform and a search engine. Proficiency in utilizing its search engine functionality can significantly enhance one's success on the social platform.

CHAPTER 5

Harnessing Hashtags: The Untold Strategy for Video Discoverability

Hashtags, commonly found on platforms such as Twitter and Instagram, have played a significant role on YouTube, although their impact has often gone unnoticed. Although YouTube initially did not adopt a hashtag-centric model, it eventually acknowledged the significance of hashtags and implemented them to enhance the discoverability of videos. How can one effectively utilize them to enhance their outreach? This article explores the undisclosed techniques for effectively utilizing hashtags on the YouTube platform.

Start with the fundamentals: Comprehend the operational capabilities: YouTube permits the inclusion of hashtags within the video description or title. After being added, these clickable links appear above your video title and direct users to a list of other videos that share the same hashtag.

The 'Rule of Three' states that although you can include multiple hashtags in a YouTube video, only the first three will be shown above the video title. Ensure that the initial three hashtags you include are highly pertinent and effectively encapsulate the central theme of your video.

Consider using hashtags that align with the search terms your audience is likely to use. Simpler and more intuitive hashtags, such as #TravelVlog or #VeganRecipes, are more likely to be searched compared to hashtags that are overly complex or wordy.

Branded hashtags can be created by converting unique taglines, campaign names, or channel slogans into hashtags. This not only improves brand recognition but also facilitates the discovery of all brand-related content by fans.

Stay informed about current trends by monitoring popular hashtags relevant to your content niche. Leveraging popular topics, if relevant, can enhance the visibility of your video among a wider audience.

Using a combination of broad and niche hashtags can be beneficial. Broad hashtags, such as #Fitness, have the potential to reach a larger audience. However, they also face significant competition from other users utilizing the same hashtag. Incorporating niche-specific tags, such as #HIITforBeginners, can effectively target and engage a dedicated audience for your video.

YouTube's policies explicitly prohibit the use of misleading hashtags. Using irrelevant or popular hashtags solely for the purpose of increasing views can result in the removal or penalization of your video.

Examine competitor tags. Examine the hashtags employed by competitors or prominent creators within your specific field. It is crucial to prioritize the creation of original content and the use of appropriate tags, as these practices can provide valuable insights into the preferences of the audience.

It is not always advisable to use all 15 hashtags allowed by YouTube. To optimize the visibility and target the appropriate audience, it is advisable to utilize pertinent tags and refrain from excessive tagging, which may give the impression of spamming.

Evaluate hashtag performance through YouTube Analytics for tracking and adjustment purposes. Identify the sources of highest traffic and adjust your strategy accordingly.

Exercise responsible use of hashtags: Although it may be tempting to employ controversial or sensitive hashtags for the purpose of gaining attention, it is crucial to approach this practice with a sense of responsibility. It is advisable to refrain from utilizing tags that have the potential to be perceived as harmful, deceptive, or objectionable.

To expand the reach of your videos beyond YouTube, it is advisable to employ consistent hashtags when sharing them on other platforms such as Twitter or Instagram. Consistency is crucial for establishing a cohesive online brand identity.

Engage with hashtag searches by regularly clicking on the hashtags to explore associated content. Interact with the provided videos, contribute comments, and foster a community centered on common interests.

Inform Your Audience: When introducing a novel hashtag,

provide educational content to your viewers. Promote active engagement with the platform by encouraging users to utilize, share, and generate content through video creation.

When creating content that targets a global audience, it is advisable to incorporate popular hashtags in different languages or those that are culturally relevant.

In summary, although hashtags on YouTube may not be as prevalent as on other platforms, they serve as a powerful tool for content creators seeking to increase the visibility of their videos. By strategically implementing hashtags, content can effectively reach a broader and more relevant audience. Embrace the utilization of hashtags as a means to enhance the visibility and reach of your content.

CHAPTER 6

Community Tab Magic: Engaging with Your Audience Beyond Videos

Despite being overlooked by numerous creators, the You-Tube Community Tab holds untapped potential. In addition to videos, this feature provides creators with an interactive platform to engage with their audience, share updates, collect feedback, and perform other activities. Utilizing the Community Tab can enhance both subscriber engagement and overall channel performance. Here is a comprehensive guide to effectively utilizing its capabilities.

Exploring the Community Tab: The Community Tab on YouTube serves as a social media feed exclusively accessible to channels with a minimum of 1,000 subscribers. Creators can share various types of content, such as polls, images,

GIFs, updates, and video links, on their YouTube channels. These posts are then displayed in the YouTube feeds of their subscribers.

Regular posting is important for maintaining consistency. Regular posts maintain subscriber engagement and provide timely updates. Increase the frequency of sharing personal content, such as behind-the-scenes images or shoutouts to subscribers, in order to allow your community to have a better understanding of the individual behind the camera.

The Community Tab offers the valuable feature of creating polls for gathering feedback. Request audience feedback on video topics, channel branding, or engage them with entertaining questions to gather their input.

Share Achievements: Have you reached a significant number of subscribers? Have you completed the editing process for a complex video? Please disseminate these triumphs among your community. Engaging with your audience through personalization fosters a sense of connection and inclusion.

One effective strategy to generate anticipation is to share sneak peeks and teasers of forthcoming videos. This can be achieved by posting teaser images, GIFs, or providing brief descriptions of the content. This effectively sustains audience engagement and anticipation for your content.

YouTube is a large and diverse community of creators. Please provide any videos, channels, collaborating creators, or content that you find admirable or inspiring. It promotes positivity and cultivates a sense of community.

Engage with comments by actively responding to them on

your Community Tab posts. This direct interaction enhances engagement and fosters a sense of value among subscribers.

Exclusive Content: Share exclusive behind-the-scenes content, bloopers, or snippets that are not included in the main video. This distinct content provides subscribers with a motivation to regularly visit and engage with your Community Tab.

Occasionally sharing personal anecdotes, challenges, or life updates can enhance relatability to one's audience, while still maintaining privacy.

Occasionally engage in collaborative initiatives with your audience by organizing challenges or contests that encourage subscribers to contribute content, ideas, or art. Highlight these contributions to foster a sense of community engagement with the channel.

Create Playlists: Share carefully curated playlists that organize content thematically or showcase videos from different creators centered around a specific topic.

External Link Sharing: Do you have a recently published blog post that you would like to share? Is there an upcoming event? Do you have any relevant articles to share? Publish it on the Community Tab to increase website traffic.

YouTube offers engagement metrics for monitoring Community Tab post engagement. It is important to regularly evaluate these metrics in order to gain insights into the preferences and interests of your audience.

Encourage Cross-Platform Engagement: It is important to strike a balance, but occasionally guide your YouTube audience to your other social media platforms, facilitating their ability to engage with you across various digital channels.

Commemorate Your Community: Allocate posts to express gratitude and celebrate your community. Gestures such as acknowledging a subscriber's birthday, featuring fan art, or giving random shoutouts contribute to the development of loyalty.

In conclusion, although videos are central to YouTube, the Community Tab provides a valuable platform for establishing personal connections. As the digital environment becomes more saturated, channels that can cultivate authentic community engagement will distinguish themselves. Explore the profound potential of the Community Tab to foster authentic connections on your channel, transcending mere content creation.

CHAPTER 7

The Perfect Video Description: Boosting Discoverability and Providing Value

The video description box on YouTube is frequently overlooked, but it presents valuable opportunities. An optimized description enhances a video's discoverability and provides an opportunity to engage with viewers, offer supplementary materials, and promote other content. Creating an optimal description necessitates a skill in captivating the viewers and adhering to the YouTube algorithm. This guide provides a comprehensive overview of how to effectively master both skills.

The initial three lines hold significance. The opening lines of your description are of utmost importance as they are visible to users without the need to click on "show more." Revise these lines to be concise, engaging, and relevant to the video. Please provide the primary keywords for SEO purposes.

Keyword optimization refers to the process of strategically selecting and incorporating relevant keywords into a piece of content in order to improve its visibility and ranking in search engine results. The description of a video should be optimized with relevant keywords, similar to the video title and tags. Utilize tools such as Google's Keyword Planner, TubeBuddy, or vidIQ for the purpose of identifying high-ranking keywords. Please ensure that the sentences are concise and written in an academic style while maintaining a natural flow within the text.

Enhance the Video's Worth: Elaborate on the content of your video within the description. If the content is a tutorial, please offer a concise and structured set of instructions. For vlogs, provide a concise narrative structure. This not only enhances the content's worth but also increases its volume, which can be advantageous for search engine optimization (SEO).

Include links to other related videos or playlists to enhance promotion and engagement with your content. By incorporating links, you enhance the value for viewers and enhance the likelihood of prolonged viewing duration on your channel.

CTAs, also known as Call to Actions, are prompts or directives that encourage users to take a specific action. Kindly encourage viewers to engage with the content by expressing their support through actions such as liking, sharing, commenting, or subscribing. Although CTAs are often included in videos, their effectiveness can be enhanced by also including them in the video description.

To enhance user experience, it is advisable to include time-stamps for distinct sections in videos exceeding a duration of 10 minutes. Segmented navigation enhances user experience by allowing viewers to navigate directly to specific segments that align with their interests.

External links and resources should be included in the video description if they have been referenced. This includes sources, studies, products, or any other relevant resources. The inclusion of a resource hub enhances credibility and provides a valuable source of information for viewers.

Include links to your social media profiles, website, or blog to promote your other online platforms. It contributes to the development of a comprehensive online presence.

When promoting products using affiliate links, it is important to ensure transparency by including them in a clear and straightforward manner. Furthermore, it is essential to incorporate a transparent disclaimer regarding any affiliations or partnerships with third-party entities in order to uphold the trust and credibility of your audience.

Credits and Acknowledgments: It is important to provide appropriate credits if your video involves collaborations, includes music, or incorporates third-party content. Engaging in ethical behavior not only fosters strong professional relationships but also upholds moral principles.

Consistent formatting of video descriptions enhances the professional and organized appearance of your channel. It is advisable to develop a standardized template that can be tailored to individual videos.

Encourage Comment Engagement: Conclude your video description by incorporating a question or discussion prompt pertaining to the content presented. This can stimulate discussions in the comments section, thereby enhancing user engagement.

When sharing multiple links, it is advisable to use URL shorteners such as Bit.ly to maintain a tidy description. It is important to ensure that the destinations of these links are clearly visible in order to prevent any potential mistrust.

Revise outdated descriptions. Periodically review descriptions of popular vintage videos. Sharing new links or information can increase traffic to your latest content.

To remain informed about YouTube's guidelines, please ensure you stay updated. YouTube has established guidelines regarding deceptive descriptions, spam, and other forms of inappropriate content. It is important to regularly review these descriptions to ensure compliance.

In conclusion, the visual and auditory content of a video remains paramount on YouTube. However, the description serves as a supplementary tool that, when utilized effectively, can significantly enhance the reach and value of the content. The website acts as a connection between the content and potential viewers. A strong and appealing website can handle higher levels of traffic. Craft your descriptions carefully to enhance discoverability and viewer engagement.

CHAPTER 8

Call-to-Action Best Practices: Guiding Viewer Behavior

A call-to-action (CTA) is a prompt that motivates users to perform a particular action, such as subscribing to a channel, sharing a video, or clicking on a link. CTAs are of utmost importance on platforms such as YouTube, where viewer engagement plays a critical role in determining the visibility of content. This analysis delves into the optimal strategies for creating impactful calls-to-action (CTAs) that effectively influence viewer behavior while avoiding an overly assertive approach.

Please rewrite the user's text to be concise and academic. Ensure that your communication is precise and unambiguous, providing explicit details and avoiding any vagueness or ambiguity. Unclear calls-to-action (CTAs) can cause confusion among users. Instead of stating "Check out our content," it is recommended to use the phrase "Click below to watch our latest tutorial." Being direct typically leads to more favorable outcomes.

Emphasize a Singular Key Action: Although it may be tempting to request viewers to engage in multiple actions simultaneously, overwhelming them can result in a state of inaction. It is recommended to prioritize a single primary call-to-action (CTA) in each video, even if you mention additional CTAs.

Strategically place CTAs in videos, considering both the beginning and end as popular options, while also taking into account the video's context. A mid-video call-to-action (CTA) can be highly effective, particularly when it is contextually relevant.

Utilize visual aids such as on-screen graphics, annotations, or end screens to supplement verbal calls-to-action (CTAs). Visual stimuli can enhance the probability of the intended behavior.

Utilize emotional appeal to evoke viewers' emotions. When soliciting donations for a cause, it is effective to provide a compelling narrative or relevant statistic to inspire potential donors to contribute.

To encourage viewers to take action, it is important to offer immediate value such as a discount, a freebie, or exclusive content. Ensure that the effort or investment is worthwhile for them.

Encourage Community Engagement: Rather than simply requesting viewers to "subscribe," extend an invitation for them to "participate in the community." This promotes a feeling of inclusion.

Encourage viewer engagement by inviting them to express their opinions, share personal anecdotes, or respond to a specific question in the comments section. Effective calls-to-action (CTAs) result in an active comment section, thereby increasing video engagement.

Conduct testing and analysis. YouTube Analytics can be utilized to track and evaluate the efficacy of various call-to-action (CTA) strategies. Modify the approach according to the prompts that produce optimal outcomes.

Maintaining authenticity is crucial as viewers possess the ability to detect insincerity. To maintain authenticity and brand consistency, it is advisable to refrain from using exaggerated appeals and to ensure that your call-to-action (CTA) is sincere.

Excessive choices can overwhelm viewers, therefore it is advisable to limit the number of options provided. When presenting multiple calls-to-action (CTAs), it is advisable to restrict their number to two or three.

Establishing Urgency: Utilizing phrases such as "for a limited time" or "before it expires" generates a perception of urgency, motivating individuals to take prompt action.

Simplify the desired action for viewers to facilitate ease of execution. Verify that the provided link is both functional and accessible. For sign-up procedures, it is important to ensure simplicity and ease of use.

Emphasize the Advantages: Reinforce the viewers' awareness of the positive outcomes associated with engaging in the desired course of action. What type of content can subscribers anticipate if they choose to subscribe? How does sharing benefit individuals and communities?

Respecting viewer autonomy is crucial when using CTAs as behavior-guiding tools. It is advisable to refrain from exhibiting excessive aggression and to consistently demonstrate gratitude for any actions undertaken.

In essence, a successful call-to-action (CTA) requires a careful equilibrium between persuasive techniques and respectful communication, as well as a balance between providing guidance and allowing individuals to make their own choices. The request is framed as an invitation rather than an imposition. By considering the target audience and providing meaningful content, creators can create effective calls-to-action (CTAs) that not only increase viewer engagement but also strengthen the relationship between the creator and the viewer. Adopt these recommended strategies and utilize your CTAs as a means to foster a more active and lively community.

CHAPTER 9

Optimizing Video Length: Finding the Sweet Spot for Engagement

YouTube creators often grapple with the perennial query regarding the optimal duration of their videos: What is the ideal length for my video? The impact of video length on viewer engagement, retention rates, and content promotion through algorithms varies and does not have a universal answer. This guide provides detailed instructions for optimizing video length to achieve optimal engagement.

It is important to have a clear understanding of your audience. Audience preferences may vary, so it is important to consider this before discussing specific details. Younger individuals may have a preference for concise and dynamic content, whereas older individuals may be more inclined towards longer and detailed videos. Understanding the behavior of your target audience is the initial stage.

The Value Proposition: Primarily, your content should offer substantial value. To maximize viewer engagement, it is crucial to ensure that every second of a tutorial or documentary, regardless of its duration, provides valuable content. Minimize unnecessary and extraneous information.

YouTube Analytics is a valuable tool for content creators. Examine your Audience Retention metrics thoroughly. Early drop-off of viewers may suggest that the length of your introductions is excessive. A sudden decrease in engagement may indicate that a particular segment was not captivating. Utilize the provided data for necessary adjustments.

The Algorithmic Perspective: YouTube prioritizes longer watch times and high retention rates. A 5-minute video with 80% retention is preferable to a 10-minute video with 40% retention.

The 7-15 minute duration is often considered ideal for various types of content, particularly educational or entertainment videos. The text is of sufficient length for thorough exploration while also being concise enough to maintain reader engagement.

Implement search engine optimization techniques to improve the visibility and ranking of your website in search engine results. When focusing on popular search queries with high search volumes, such as "How to tie a tie," it is important to understand that searchers are seeking prompt and concise responses. Shorter videos tend to have better performance in these situations.

Consider dividing your lengthy content into parts or series

if it is appropriate for the nature of the content. This feature has the potential to generate anticipation and guide viewers to subsequent videos, thereby enhancing overall viewing duration.

Engagement hooks are consistently present throughout the text. To maintain viewer engagement, it is important to consistently incorporate engagement hooks such as thought-provoking questions, enticing teasers, or captivating visuals, regardless of the length of the content.

Respecting the time of viewers. It is important to consistently value and prioritize the time of the audience. Avoid extending the duration of a task to 10 minutes solely to meet a length requirement if it can be effectively completed in 5 minutes while still providing value.

Engage in experimentation and adaptation: Embrace the opportunity to explore various video lengths. Conduct a performance analysis and make necessary adjustments in response to feedback and data.

Platform Considerations: It is important to note that YouTube is not the sole platform to be considered. When cross-posting, it is important to consider the platform norms and adjust the video length accordingly. For instance, videos posted on Instagram should be shorter, while those on YouTube can be longer.

For videos that are longer than 10 minutes, it is advisable to incorporate timestamps to indicate different sections. It improves user experience by enabling viewers to navigate to specific segments of interest.

Staying informed about trends and virality is important. Occasionally, the duration of videos is influenced by viral challenges or formats, and capitalizing on this trend can lead to favorable outcomes.

When aiming for monetization, it is important to note that videos exceeding 8 minutes in length can accommodate multiple ad placements. Nevertheless, it is important to consider the potential trade-off of reduced viewer retention.

The optimal video length may vary due to evolving algorithms, audience preferences, and content strategies. Maintain adaptability and consistently prioritize the delivery of value.

In conclusion, video length is an important factor to consider, but it should be viewed as just one component of the overall picture. The content's essence, delivery, and value are equally, if not more, significant. To effectively engage your audience and optimize your content's visibility on YouTube, it is important to determine an appropriate length that aligns with your content's objectives. Striking the right balance will ensure that your content resonates well with both your viewers and the YouTube algorithm.

CHAPTER 10

Consistency is Key: How Regular Uploads Drive Growth

Consistency is crucial in the dynamic digital landscape of YouTube. Consistent uploads are crucial for the success of a channel. What is the reason behind this phenomenon? This analysis examines the impact of consistency on YouTube and its role in driving channel growth.

Creating Audience Expectation: Consider your preferred television program. The television show is scheduled to be broadcasted every Tuesday at 8 PM, and you eagerly await its airing. Consistent uploading establishes a predictable schedule for viewers, which in turn promotes loyalty and encourages repeat visits.

YouTube's algorithm prioritizes channels that effectively engage users and encourage them to spend more time on the platform. Consistently uploading content on YouTube indicates to the platform that your channel is actively engaged and plays a role in retaining users.

Creating a Content Library: Uploading more content expands the size of your video library. Over time, the likelihood of viewers discovering your channel through search queries and video recommendations increases.

Momentum and growth are facilitated by each video, as it presents a fresh opportunity to engage and attract new subscribers. Regularly uploading videos helps to sustain momentum and increases the likelihood of attracting new viewers who may be introduced to your content through each individual video.

Regular uploads facilitate a continuous feedback loop with the audience. Engagement metrics such as comments, likes, and shares on each video offer valuable insights into audience preferences, enabling the refinement and enhancement of future content.

In fields such as education or reviews, consistency plays a crucial role in establishing credibility. Consistently posting on a specific topic enhances your perceived authority and establishes you as a reliable source within that field.

Consistency in uploading content plays a crucial role in fostering community building and viewer engagement. By regularly interacting with viewers through consistent uploads, a sense of community is developed, leading to the transformation of passive viewers into active advocates for the channel.

Habitual Viewing: Humans exhibit habitual behavior. Consistent content release schedules can cultivate a sense of anticipation and habit among viewers, integrating video consumption into their regular routines.

Subscriber attrition is a common occurrence across all channels. Regular uploads can mitigate this attrition by consistently attracting new subscribers.

Increasing Revenue Potential: Channels that monetize can capitalize on additional uploads to generate more views and ad placements, thereby enhancing their revenue.

Consistent uploading enables creators to promptly adapt to trends, changes, or feedback. Agility is essential for maintaining relevance.

Maintaining a regular upload schedule instills discipline and facilitates skill improvement for content creators. Consistent practice leads to continuous improvement in one's craft, resulting in the production of higher quality content over time.

Challenges and considerations:

Consistency is crucial, but it should be approached with mindfulness.

The emphasis should be on producing a smaller number of high-quality videos rather than a larger quantity of mediocre ones. Achieving a balance is essential.

Regularly uploading content can lead to burnout. Efficient workload management can be achieved through strategies such as batch production of content or scheduling regular breaks.

Maintaining Authenticity: Consistency should not compromise authenticity. It is important to prioritize authentic content over strictly adhering to a predetermined schedule.

In conclusion, maintaining a regular uploading schedule on YouTube has various benefits, including promoting growth, fostering community engagement, and establishing credibility. However, the effectiveness of any tool depends on how it is used. Creators can maximize the potential of the platform by comprehending its subtleties and maintaining a harmonious equilibrium between consistency, quality, and authenticity. This approach guarantees long-term growth and achievement.

CHAPTER 11

Collaborations & Partnerships: Multiply Your Reach

The significance of collaboration within the YouTube ecosystem is immense. Collaboration between multiple creators or brands frequently results in the creation of content that appeals to a wider audience, resulting in significant growth and a more varied viewership. This chapter examines the complexities of collaborations and partnerships and their potential to significantly expand one's reach.

In the realm of YouTube, creators frequently discover that collaborating rather than competing fosters mutual growth. When two channels collaborate, they mutually expose their audiences to one another, creating a mutually beneficial outcome.

Collaborations enable creators to explore content beyond their typical areas of focus. A collaboration between a cooking channel and a travel vlogger can result in a distinctive series that explores the intersection of cuisine and culture.

Collaboration leads to increased exposure as it allows for the sharing of content across various platforms and channels. This exposure has the potential to attract a larger number of new subscribers and viewers, thereby increasing discoverability.

Collaborating with fellow creators can facilitate personal growth and learning opportunities. One can acquire new skills, techniques, or insights related to content creation, audience engagement, and channel management.

Partnering with established creators or brands can enhance the credibility of your channel. Receiving an endorsement or being featured by a reputable individual can enhance the reputation of your channel.

Collaborations typically involve the sharing of resources, such as equipment, locations, or production teams. This may result in increased production value and enhanced content quality.

Brand collaborations are a common practice where brands form partnerships with YouTube creators for promotional purposes. Collaborations can be profitable, but it is important to ensure that the brand aligns with the values and audience of your channel.

Steps for Effective Collaborations:

Select suitable partners whose content, style, and target audience are compatible with your own. The experience should be natural, rather than contrived.

Clear communication is essential for a successful collaboration. It is important to discuss goals, expectations, roles, and responsibilities in advance. This will help to establish a common understanding and ensure a smooth working relationship.

Co-promotion involves the active promotion of the collaboration by both parties through various means such as teasers, social media shout-outs, and community posts.

Mutual respect entails valuing the ideas, audience, and brand of fellow creators. Successful collaborations rely on mutual appreciation and respect.

Ensure equal prominence for all collaborators in the content to share the spotlight. This equilibrium guarantees that all audiences perceive a sense of worth.

Monitor audience feedback to gauge their reactions. Participants frequently offer feedback regarding their preferences, areas of dissatisfaction, and suggestions for potential future collaborations.

Legal considerations, particularly in brand partnerships, necessitate the establishment of unambiguous contractual agreements. To avoid potential disputes in the future, it is important to establish clear guidelines regarding deliverables, payments, rights, and other critical aspects.

Authenticity is crucial when engaging in collaborations, despite the many benefits they offer. Engage in collaborative projects that align with your interests and genuinely connect with your target audience.

In conclusion, collaborations and partnerships serve as valuable assets for YouTube creators. They provide a distinctive combination of diversified content, engaged audience, and rapid growth. By implementing a strategic approach, effective communication, and a touch of creativity, content creators can significantly expand their audience, elevating their channels to unprecedented levels of success.

CHAPTER 12

YouTube Analytics Deep Dive: Understanding What Works

To succeed on YouTube, creators must produce high-quality content and possess a comprehensive understanding of the metrics that contribute to its success. YouTube Analytics provides a wealth of data, offering valuable insights into viewer behavior, content performance, and areas for potential improvement. This chapter provides guidance on navigating YouTube Analytics to determine effective strategies for your channel.

Dashboard Overview: Upon accessing the Analytics section within YouTube Studio, users are presented with a concise summary that provides a snapshot of their channel's performance. This encompasses metrics such as views, watch time, subscriber count, and estimated revenue.

Real-time metrics provide an overview of video performance within the past 48 hours. Tracking the immediate response to a newly uploaded video is highly valuable.

The metrics of watch time and views provide information on the frequency and duration of video consumption. A discrepancy between high view count and low watch time may suggest the presence of attention-grabbing titles and thumbnails, but a lack of engaging content that fails to retain viewers.

Audience retention is a critical metric that indicates the average percentage of a video that viewers watch. Spikes in viewership data can indicate segments that were rewatched, whereas dips may suggest portions that were skipped by viewers.

Engagement metrics, such as likes, comments, shares, and subscribers, reflect the level of audience interaction with your content. A video's high engagement is indicative of its successful resonance with viewers.

Traffic Source Types can help identify the origins of views, including direct searches, suggested videos, external sources, and more. This can inform and shape your promotional strategies.

Demographics encompass factors such as age, gender, geographic location, and device preference, which are crucial for understanding your audience. Customize your content to effectively reach the majority of your target audience or to specifically target particular segments.

Impressions and Click-Through Rate (CTR) are two

metrics used to measure the performance of video thumbnails. Impressions represent the frequency at which these thumbnails are displayed to viewers, while CTR measures the proportion of impressions that result in views. A high number of impressions coupled with a low click-through rate (CTR) may indicate that the thumbnail or title of your content lacks sufficient appeal.

Earnings and monetization metrics. For channels that are monetized, it is important to provide a comprehensive analysis of the various sources of revenue, such as advertisements, channel memberships, and revenue from YouTube Premium.

Playback Locations: Determine the platforms and sources through which viewers access your content, including YouTube, embedded sites, and other channels.

Video Performance Analysis: Evaluate the highest-performing videos within a specified time period. This tool can assist in developing a content strategy by identifying the most effective topics or styles.

Effective Analytics Strategies:

Regularly reviewing your analytics is essential. Regular check-ins on a weekly basis can assist in maintaining awareness of the current state and trends of your channel.

A/B Testing involves conducting experiments with various video styles, thumbnails, or titles, and utilizing analytics to identify the most effective approach.

Adapt and evolve by producing more content that aligns with popular content types or topics indicated by data analysis.

Identify and rectify weak points: In the event of decreased audience retention or underperformance of specific videos, it is important to analyze the reasons behind these issues and take appropriate measures to address them in future uploads.

Establishing clear goals is essential. Establishing specific, measurable goals based on data is essential for guiding content creation and promotional strategies. These goals may include increasing watch time, improving click-through rates (CTR), or enhancing audience engagement.

In conclusion, YouTube Analytics encompasses more than mere numerical data and visual representations. This narrative explores the trajectory of your content, including its successes, challenges, and its impact on the extensive YouTube community. Through thorough analysis of this data, content creators can uncover intricate success patterns, enhancing their strategies and guaranteeing that their content not only reaches but also captivates their intended audience.

CHAPTER 13

The Importance of Audience Retention: Keeping Viewers Hooked

In the dynamic realm of YouTube, capturing a viewer's attention is a significant hurdle, while sustaining their engagement poses a true test. Audience Retention is a crucial metric in YouTube Analytics that serves as an indicator of the level of engagement your content has achieved. This chapter examines the significance of audience retention and provides strategies for maintaining viewer engagement throughout a presentation.

The study of audience retention. Audience retention refers to the average percentage of a video that is viewed by viewers. A retention rate of 70% for a 10-minute video implies that, on average, viewers watched 7 minutes of the video. High retention rates indicate that viewers found the content engaging and valuable, while low retention rates may suggest a loss of interest or a failure to find the desired information.

The Significance of Retention

YouTube's algorithm prioritizes videos that have high viewer retention. YouTube is more inclined to recommend videos to other users when they watch a significant portion or the entirety of the video.

Increased watch time can result in higher ad revenue for monetized channels.

Increased retention rates can enhance the credibility of your content, leading to greater trust and potential investment from viewers, collaborators, and sponsors.

Retention is influenced by various factors.

High-quality, thoroughly researched content is more likely to engage and retain viewers.

Pacing is a critical factor in video production as it can significantly impact viewer engagement. If a video is excessively slow, it may lead to viewer boredom, while a video that is excessively fast can overwhelm the audience.

It is important to ensure that the content of your video is relevant to its title and thumbnail in order to avoid misleading viewers.

Engagement can be enhanced by incorporating visual aids such as graphics, B-rolls, animations, and interactive elements like polls.

Methods to Enhance Audience Retention:

The initial 15 seconds of a video are crucial for capturing the viewer's attention. Begin with an engaging introduction that captivates the reader's interest, employing a thought-provoking question, an intriguing teaser, or a bold assertion, in order to stimulate curiosity.

Storyboarding and structuring: Develop a plan for the sequential progression of your video. A video that is well-organized, with distinct segments or chapters, can effectively lead viewers from one point to another without interruption.

The Importance of Accurate Thumbnails and Titles in Engaging Viewers: While thumbnails and titles are effective in attracting clicks, it is crucial to ensure that they accurately depict the content of the video in order to retain viewers.

Interactive content can effectively engage viewers through various means such as posing questions, conducting polls, or encouraging them to comment. This engagement can foster viewer engagement, thereby enhancing their propensity to sustain their viewership for a longer duration.

Regularly assess and consider audience comments and feedback. Consider viewer feedback regarding segments that are perceived as lengthy, uninteresting, or perplexing, and incorporate this input when creating future content.

Consistent visuals and branding contribute to a familiar and comfortable viewing experience for viewers.

Employing cards and end screens strategically can enhance channel retention by suggesting related content or directing viewers to another video.

To optimize video length, it is recommended to conduct tests with various durations and assess audience retention to determine the most effective option.

To minimize distractions, it is important to ensure that the audio and visuals of your video are clear and steady, and that there are minimal disruptive elements present. Ensuring a seamless viewing experience is crucial for viewer retention.

In the realm of YouTube, it is crucial to prioritize the retention of viewer attention. The intended recipients of a message or communication. Retention serves as more than just a metric, as it demonstrates the capacity of content to engage, educate, and entertain. By recognizing the significance of content and employing effective strategies to improve it, creators can ensure that their content is not only viewed but also genuinely experienced. This can result in the development of a loyal audience and long-term success for their channel.

CHAPTER 14

Interactive Features: Polls, Cards, and End Screens

Engaging the audience involves both delivering compelling content and fostering interactive experiences. YouTube offers various interactive features that aim to engage viewers, guide them to additional content, and collect feedback. This chapter will discuss the effective utilization of Polls, Cards, and End Screens, which form a powerful trio.

Polls are surveys conducted to gather information or opinions from a specific group of people. Polls are a means by which creators can solicit direct feedback from viewers within a video.

What are the reasons for their utilization?

Audience engagement refers to the active participation of viewers in interacting with the content.

• Soliciting Feedback: Assessing viewpoints on particular

subjects or making decisions regarding future content based on viewer preferences.

What are the most effective ways to utilize them?

• Pertinent Inquiries: Pose questions that pertain to the video's subject matter or the overarching theme of your channel.

• Optimal Timing: Incorporate polls strategically during appropriate junctures to ensure minimal disruption to the video's continuity.

What is the definition of cards? Cards are interactive panels that can be triggered to appear at any given moment within a video. They have the ability to advertise additional content, channels, or websites.

What are the reasons for their usage?

Content promotion involves directing viewers to other videos, playlists, or channels.

External links on eligible channels' cards can direct users to external sites, crowdfunding platforms, or merchandise sites.

What are the most effective ways to utilize them?

Strategic timing involves introducing cards during relevant moments of discussion to enhance click-through rates.

Excessive use or frequent placement of cards can cause distraction and annoyance to viewers, thus minimizing their effectiveness as a tool for engagement.

End screens refer to the elements that appear at the end of a video on platforms such as YouTube. They typically include clickable elements such as buttons or links that allow viewers to take specific actions, such as subscribing to a channel, watching another video, or visiting a website. End screens are typically displayed during the final 5-20 seconds of a video.

The promotional options available include videos, playlists, a subscribe button, or another channel, with a maximum limit of four elements.

What are the reasons for their utilization?

Channel growth can be achieved by encouraging viewers to subscribe and explore additional content, thereby enhancing the overall viewership and engagement of the channel.

Viewer retention can be increased by suggesting additional videos, which encourages viewers to stay within the channel's ecosystem for a longer duration.

What are the most effective ways to utilize them?

• Appropriate Recommendations: To enhance viewer engagement, it is recommended to promote content that is relevant to the video they have just watched, thereby ensuring their sustained interest.

• Utilize clear and explicit calls-to-action by incorporating verbal or textual prompts to motivate viewers to click, in addition to the end screen.

Best practices for interactive features:

• Visual Appeal: Ensure that all interactive elements are aesthetically pleasing and consistent with the visual design of your video and channel.

Utilize YouTube Analytics to assess viewer engagement with these features. If a card is not receiving sufficient clicks, it is advisable to reassess both its content and placement.

YouTube frequently releases updates and implements changes to its features. To maximize the benefits of the platform, it is important to stay well-informed.

In conclusion, the strategic utilization of YouTube's interactive features has the potential to significantly increase viewer engagement and promote the growth of channels. They serve as a connection between the creator and the viewer, converting a passive viewing experience into an interactive one. Creators can enhance their relationship with their audience and achieve channel success by utilizing polls, cards, and end screens to drive engagement and retention.

CHAPTER 15

Elevate Your Content with High-Quality Production

Producing content for YouTube entails more than simply having a good idea; it involves effectively conveying that idea with a high level of polish and professionalism. Producing content of superior quality can differentiate oneself from other creators, leading to a competitive advantage and improving the overall viewer experience. This chapter aims to provide insights into techniques and strategies for enhancing the quality of your content through high-level production.

Production value is the viewer's perception of the overall quality of a video. The factors that contribute to the overall quality of a multimedia production include visual clarity, sound quality, editing proficiency, and presentation.

Enhancing Visual Quality: • Acquire High-Quality Equipment: Although using a smartphone is acceptable initially, it is advisable to upgrade to a DSLR or mirrorless camera as your channel expands.

The use of studio lights can contribute to the creation of consistent and controlled environments, complementing the benefits of natural light. The use of softboxes or ring lights can have a substantial impact.

To achieve stabilization in video recording, it is recommended to employ tripods, gimbals, or stabilizers in order to minimize the occurrence of shaky footage. Stable shots contribute to a heightened sense of professionalism.

When composing a photograph, it is important to adhere to the rule of thirds, maintain appropriate framing, and avoid cluttered backgrounds.

Sound Clarity: • External microphones are typically superior to built-in microphones. Lapel microphones, shotgun microphones, and condenser microphones have the potential to significantly enhance the quality of audio recordings.

Soundproofing techniques, such as incorporating soft furnishings or foam panels, can effectively minimize echo and undesired noise in a recording room.

Post-production involves utilizing software such as Audacity or Adobe Audition to reduce noise and enhance audio quality.

Advanced editing options are available through software tools such as Adobe Premiere Pro, Final Cut Pro, or DaVinci Resolve.

Utilize cuts and transitions with intention. It is advisable to refrain from excessive use of flashy transitions, as a simple cut can often be more effective.

Enhance your videos by incorporating vibrant graphics, titles, and animations.

Color grading is a technique used to enhance the mood and aesthetics of a video by giving it a unique visual appearance.

Planning and storyboarding are essential steps in the creative process.

Pre-production involves the process of strategizing and organizing the content. Scripting and storyboarding are valuable tools that help facilitate the shooting process by ensuring the inclusion of all necessary shots.

Engaging introductions are crucial as they have the potential to influence a viewer's decision to continue watching within the first few seconds. Craft engaging introductions that provide a glimpse into the video's worth.

Engagement enhancers

B-Rolls refer to additional footage that is edited together with the primary shot. B-rolls serve various purposes such as illustrating a point, alleviating monotony, or enhancing storytelling.

Utilize features such as polls, cards, and end screens to enhance viewer engagement and create an interactive viewing experience, as previously mentioned.

It is important to remain informed and engage in ongoing training.

Production techniques are subject to evolution. Workshops and tutorials are available to help individuals stay updated with these advancements. Participate in online workshops or access tutorials to enhance your skills.

• Utilize feedback loops to regularly solicit input from

peers or mentors. An external perspective can identify areas of improvement.

In conclusion, it is not necessary to have a large budget like Hollywood in order to achieve high-quality production. Minor adjustments in lighting, sound, or editing have the potential to significantly enhance the quality of your content, elevating it from amateur to professional. Although production value is important, the content holds greater significance. The key to achieving success on YouTube is to combine engaging content with high-quality production. As audience demand for high-quality content rises, allocating resources and effort towards improving production can result in substantial benefits in terms of audience size, interaction, and channel expansion.

CHAPTER 16

Community Building: Fostering Loyalty and Super Fans

YouTube is not just a video platform, but rather a dynamic community where creators and viewers engage, collaborate, and progress collectively. In this context, establishing a strong community is not only advantageous but also indispensable. A devoted community is crucial for the success of a YouTube channel. This chapter explores the strategies and techniques involved in building a community, cultivating loyalty, and nurturing devoted fans.

The Significance of Community Understanding Developing a robust community entails more than merely acquiring a base of subscribers. It refers to the creation of an environment that fosters a sense of connection, engagement, and value among viewers.

Benefits include:

Sustainable growth is achieved through the presence of a loyal community, which remains constant despite changing algorithms and trends, resulting in consistent views and engagement.

Regular interactions offer valuable feedback, contributing to the improvement of content quality and direction.

Brand ambassadors are individuals who are loyal to a brand and actively promote its content, thereby facilitating organic growth.

Engaging with your audience involves regularly interacting with them by responding to comments, participating in discussions, and acknowledging feedback.

Live streaming can enhance viewer engagement by creating real-time interactions, fostering a sense of connection.

Q&A sessions in the form of periodic videos can effectively address viewer queries, thereby fostering a sense of being heard and valued among the audience.

Consistent content delivery is essential for establishing loyalty, as it is based on trust. Consistency and high-quality content are essential for establishing reliability, which forms the basis for fostering loyalty.

Establish a secure environment.

Moderation is essential in actively monitoring and filtering comments to eliminate negative and disruptive behavior, thereby creating a positive and inclusive community environment.

Community Guidelines should provide a clear delineation of acceptable and unacceptable behavior. Adhere to these regulations and promote their observance within your community.

Recognizing and rewarding loyalty can be achieved through shoutouts, where engaged subscribers are acknowledged in videos or descriptions.

Provide loyal subscribers with exclusive content, early access, or behind-the-scenes glimpses.

Merchandise discounts can serve as a tangible expression of gratitude for channels engaged in merchandise sales.

Extend community engagement beyond YouTube by utilizing other social media platforms and organizing offline meetups.

Foster a dedicated fan base: Super Fans are individuals who exhibit exceptional levels of loyalty and engagement. They engage with your content by watching, liking, sharing, commenting, and actively promoting it.

Strategies for Cultivating Dedicated Supporters:

Patreon and similar platforms enable creators to establish exclusive communities, granting Super Fans enhanced access and content.

Personal interaction, such as direct messages or personalized thank you notes, can strengthen the loyalty of Super Fans.

Super Fans' contributions are valuable due to their ability to provide insightful feedback. Appreciate, take action, and recognize their impact on the growth of your channel.

In conclusion, the process of community building is characterized by a greater emphasis on artistic elements rather than scientific principles. The focus is on fostering authentic engagement, providing continuous value, and establishing an inclusive environment that cultivates a sense of belonging among viewers. In the current era of digital content abundance, loyalty is highly valued. Investing in community-building allows creators to achieve sustained growth and cultivate a sense of purpose, enhancing the overall satisfaction and fulfillment of their YouTube journey.

CHAPTER 17

Diversifying Monetization: Beyond YouTube Ad Revenue

The YouTube Partner Program offers creators the opportunity to monetize their channels by generating ad revenue, making it an advantageous initial step in the process. As the platform develops and competition increases, it becomes essential to diversify income sources rather than just being a wise decision. A diversified revenue stream can effectively withstand platform changes, algorithm adjustments, and demonetization challenges. This chapter examines alternative monetization strategies that go beyond the conventional revenue generated from YouTube advertisements.

The Importance of Diversification

Platform volatility refers to the potential impact on ad revenue caused by algorithm changes or policy updates.

One risk of demonetization is the potential flagging of

content as unsuitable for advertisers, resulting in a loss of potential earnings.

Fans have diverse preferences when it comes to supporting creators in order to maximize their potential. Providing diverse options accommodates the diverse audience.

Affiliate marketing refers to a marketing strategy where individuals or businesses promote products or services on behalf of another company, known as the affiliate, in exchange for a commission. Earning commissions by promoting and facilitating sales of products through provided links.

Best practices involve promoting products that are relevant to the content and audience. It is essential to consistently disclose affiliate links in order to uphold trust.

YouTube's merchandise shelf feature enables integration with platforms such as Teespring, facilitating the direct showcasing of products for sale.

Create merchandise that aligns with your brand and appeals to your community, including items such as T-shirts and customized gadgets.

Channel memberships are a feature on YouTube that allows viewers to pay a monthly fee to support their favorite creators. In return, members receive various perks such as exclusive badges, emojis, and

Exclusive benefits can be provided to subscribers who become paying members of your channel. These benefits may include badges, custom emojis, exclusive live chats, or videos.

Memberships can enhance the connection with highly devoted fans by providing increased opportunities for direct engagement.

Sponsored Content: • Brand Partnerships: Engage in

collaborations with brands to generate content centered on their products or services. It is important to maintain transparency with viewers regarding sponsorships.

Select sponsorships that are authentic and align with your content and target audience to ensure genuine integration.

Paid promotions and shoutouts involve smaller creators paying for a mention or shoutout on a larger channel to gain visibility among a larger audience.

• Uphold Integrity: Promote only content that aligns with your beliefs to safeguard the trust of your audience.

Online Courses & Workshops: Utilize your expertise by providing paid courses, workshops, or webinars in your specific field.

Platforms such as Udemy, Teachable, and Patreon can be utilized to host and monetize courses.

Crowdfunding and donations can be facilitated through platforms such as Patreon and Ko-fi, which provide opportunities for fans to financially support an artist's work through one-time or recurring contributions.

To encourage support, provide exclusive rewards such as unique content, behind-the-scenes access, or additional benefits for patrons.

In this section, we will discuss the process of licensing your content. Licensing refers to granting permission to others to use your content in specific ways, while still retaining ownership of the content. By licensing your content, you can

Viral content has the potential to attract the attention of media agencies who may want to license it for various purposes such as advertisements, news coverage, or other broadcasts.

In conclusion, diversifying monetization methods allows creators to reduce their dependence on the YouTube platform and mitigate the impact of its unpredictable changes. By diversifying their revenue streams, they can maintain the production of high-quality content without facing financial constraints, thereby establishing a sustainable and resilient channel. Furthermore, the implementation of various monetization strategies is in line with the dynamic nature of the digital ecosystem, which is characterized by constantly shifting audience preferences and consumption patterns. Creators can ensure their creative and financial growth on YouTube and beyond by being adaptive, proactive, and diversified.

CHAPTER 18

Going Live: Boosting Real-time Engagement and Growth

Live streaming is a valuable tool for creators in the dynamic realm of digital content. Live streaming not only allows for real-time interaction with viewers, but also creates a sense of immediacy and presence that cannot be replicated by pre-recorded videos. Live streaming on YouTube has the potential to enhance engagement, promote a sense of community, and accelerate the growth of a channel. This analysis explores strategies for optimizing the effectiveness of live streaming.

The Significance of Real-time Interaction:

Live sessions provide an authentic experience by showcasing creators in an unscripted and raw manner, thereby fostering a more genuine connection with the audience.

Instant feedback is facilitated through real-time commenting, allowing viewers to provide immediate feedback, ask questions, and influence the direction of the session.

Planning a live stream involves several important steps.

Purpose: Establish the objective. Are you organizing a Q&A session, commemorating an achievement, delivering a tutorial, or engaging in a discourse on recent occurrences?

To maximize attendance, it is recommended to promote the live session in advance through various channels such as videos, the community tab, or other social media platforms.

In this section, we will discuss the technical considerations that need to be taken into account.

To prevent interruptions in the streaming process, it is important to have a stable and high-speed internet connection.

Using high-quality camera and microphone equipment can enhance the viewing experience when going live, although it is possible to go live from a mobile device.

Streaming software such as OBS Studio, StreamYard, or XSplit provides enhanced control and customization options for live streaming.

Engaging the audience is an important aspect of effective communication.

Promote viewer engagement through the facilitation of questions, opinions, and participation in polls.

YouTube's Super Chat feature enables viewers to pay a nominal fee to emphasize their messages, serving as a potential revenue stream and a means to enhance viewer engagement.

Collaboration can enhance live streams by inviting other creators or guests to participate, bringing diverse perspectives and potentially expanding the reach to their respective audiences.

Monetization opportunities

Super Chat and Super Stickers enable viewers to enhance their comments by making a monetary contribution.

Exclusive membership Streams can be utilized to provide exclusive live sessions for channel members, enhancing the subscription by offering additional benefits.

Safety and moderation are important factors to consider.

• Chat Moderators: Appoint individuals who are trusted and loyal members of the community to oversee the chat and maintain a secure and constructive atmosphere.

Keyword filters can be established to automatically prevent the use of specific words or phrases that may be deemed inappropriate.

Post-stream Engagement: • Archiving: Preserve the live stream as a video on your channel to cater to individuals who were unable to attend. By employing this approach, the content consistently generates viewership and fosters active participation.

YouTube offers analytics for live sessions, allowing users to analyze and iterate their content. To enhance future streams, it is important to analyze viewer peaks, engagement metrics, and feedback.

In conclusion, live streaming is an effective method to enhance the vitality of your YouTube channel. It serves as a means of communication between content creators and viewers, effectively breaking the barrier between them in digital media. Through the effective utilization of live streaming, creators are able to establish stronger connections with their audience, enhance engagement in real-time, and expand the range of content they offer. It is crucial to approach each session with preparation and intent to ensure that it is impactful, engaging, and reflective of the channel's ethos.

CHAPTER 19

Tackling the YouTube Algorithm: What You Need to Know

The YouTube algorithm is a sophisticated and dynamic system that determines the order and selection of videos recommended to users. The algorithm has a significant impact on various aspects, such as the content displayed on a viewer's homepage feed and the recommended videos in the "Up Next" section. Understanding the operational mechanics of this algorithm is crucial for content creators who aspire to expand their channels. The following information is essential:

The YouTube Algorithm: A Comprehensive Analysis

The purpose of this study is to investigate and analyze the effects of social media usage on mental health. The primary objective of the algorithm is to maximize user engagement and retention on the platform. It accomplishes this by providing users with video recommendations that are both appealing and likely to be viewed.

The algorithm employs machine learning to analyze user behavior, taking into account factors such as video consumption, duration, and skipping patterns.

Algorithmic Consideration of Key Metrics

The algorithm places greater importance on the duration of viewer engagement rather than the number of views. A longer engagement typically suggests that the content was engaging.

The Click-Through Rate (CTR) is a metric that quantifies the frequency at which viewers click on a video after being exposed to its thumbnail. A high click-through rate (CTR) may suggest the presence of engaging thumbnails and titles.

User engagement can be measured through various indicators such as likes, comments, shares, and subscriptions, which reflect the quality of a video and the level of audience engagement.

Audience retention is enhanced when videos are able to maintain viewer engagement throughout their duration.

Creating Algorithm-friendly Content

Producing a single high-quality video that effectively engages viewers is more advantageous than creating multiple videos that are frequently skipped or abandoned.

• Stimulate Viewer Engagement: Encourage viewers to engage by liking, commenting, sharing, and subscribing. Compelling content inherently encourages engagement.

To enhance the discoverability of your videos, it is advisable to optimize the titles and descriptions by incorporating relevant keywords. However, it is important to refrain from using clickbait tactics, as they can negatively impact your metrics when viewers quickly click away from your videos.

The Significance of Consistency:

Consistent uploading schedules can indicate to the algorithm that a channel is active and dependable.

Channels that have a specific niche or topic tend to perform better as the algorithm can more effectively identify and recommend the content to a specific audience.

The Significance of Playlists:

Grouping related videos into playlists can increase viewers' watch time by encouraging them to watch multiple videos consecutively, thereby enhancing overall engagement.

Controlled recommendations can be achieved by organizing videos in a playlist, thereby influencing the sequence in which they are viewed and potentially overriding the algorithm's "Up Next" suggestions.

In order to remain informed and up-to-date, it is important to regularly seek out and access reliable sources of information. This can be achieved through various means such as reading news articles

YouTube's system, similar to Google's search algorithm, experiences regular algorithm changes. Keeping up with these changes can assist in adjusting your content strategy.

YouTube Studio offers feedback on video performance through a feedback loop. Frequent analysis of this data can provide insights into the algorithm's interpretation of your content.

Collaborations and cross-promotion are important strategies for businesses to enhance their reach and visibility. By partnering with other companies or individuals, businesses can leverage their combined resources and networks to achieve mutual benefits. This can involve joint

Collaborating with other creators can expand your content's reach by exposing it to their audience, potentially enhancing your channel's visibility in the algorithm's recommendations.

In conclusion,

Effectively navigating the YouTube algorithm does not involve attempting to manipulate or exploit its mechanisms. The key is to comprehend the objectives of the system and ensure that your content creation strategy is in line with those goals. Creators can leverage the algorithm to expand their audience and achieve continuous channel growth by prioritizing genuine engagement, delivering consistent high-quality content, and regularly analyzing performance metrics.

CHAPTER 20

Embracing Feedback: How to Use Comments Constructively

YouTube comments have both positive and negative aspects. Although they provide valuable insights, they can also generate unwarranted negativity. Feedback, whether positive or negative, is an essential tool for creators seeking growth. This chapter explores the constructive use of comments for content refinement, audience understanding, and community development.

The Significance of Feedback:

Comments offer valuable insight into the thoughts, emotions, and desires of your audience. Viewer preferences can be effectively understood through them.

Constructive feedback can identify areas for improvement, such as technical issues like audio quality, as well as provide content suggestions.

Constructive criticism involves providing actionable advice, such as suggesting improvements in lighting or recommending a deeper exploration of a specific topic.

Destructive comments encompass purely negative feedback lacking actionable advice, personal attacks, or content unrelated to the topic. It is crucial to acknowledge and determine appropriate strategies for addressing these challenges without internalizing negative emotions.

Acting on constructive feedback involves acknowledging and expressing gratitude towards the input received. This simple gesture demonstrates the appreciation for the audience's contribution, thereby promoting loyalty and engagement.

Execute modifications. If possible, and if you agree with the feedback, incorporate the suggested changes into your future content.

Follow-up: After incorporating feedback, it is advisable to demonstrate responsiveness by addressing the changes in a video or pinned comment.

When faced with destructive or negative feedback, it is important to refrain from reacting impulsively. While it is natural to feel defensive or hurt, responding immediately can exacerbate the situation or create a negative perception of oneself.

• Obtain a Second Opinion: Share your comment with a trusted individual or colleague to assess if there are any underlying constructive criticisms that you may have overlooked.

Utilize moderation tools provided by YouTube, such as comment hiding, user blocking, and term filtering. Employ these tools with discretion to uphold a favorable communal ambiance.

To encourage constructive feedback, it is recommended to ask specific questions at the end of your videos. For instance, you can prompt viewers to provide feedback on the new format by asking them how they feel about it.

Community Tab Polls allow for the use of the community tab to conduct polls or ask more comprehensive questions, offering a structured method for gathering feedback.

Gaining a Comprehensive Perspective: • Identifying Trends: While isolated comments may represent personal viewpoints, the repetition of similar sentiments among multiple viewers signifies a noteworthy trend.

In addition to comments, it is important to consider other forms of feedback such as likes, shares, watch time, and subscriber numbers. It is important to always take into account the wider range of feedback.

Fostering a Positive Community: • Emphasize Positive Interactions: Display positive or constructive comments as examples of the desired type of engagement within the community.

Establish Community Guidelines to clearly outline the desired types of comments, as well as specify the consequences, such as comment removal or user bans, for engaging in prohibited behavior.

In conclusion, feedback is a valuable tool for growth when approached with an open mind. Embracing constructive comments involves acknowledging their potential, discerning valuable insights, and utilizing them to consistently improve content and foster a dedicated and engaged community. To achieve the desired outcome of creating content that connects and adapts to the audience, it is crucial to maintain an open mindset while avoiding the influence of negative thoughts.

CHAPTER 21

Avoiding Common Pitfalls: Stay Clear of Policy Violations

Effectively navigating the YouTube platform necessitates a comprehensive understanding of both content creation and platform regulations. YouTube's policies aim to ensure a secure, inclusive, and conducive environment for both users and advertisers. Violating these guidelines may result in strikes, demonetization, or channel termination. This guide aims to help users avoid common pitfalls and ensure the successful growth of their channel without encountering any unwanted issues.

In this article, we aim to provide a comprehensive understanding of YouTube's Community Guidelines.

Please refrain from including nudity or sexually explicit content. Exercise caution and strictly adhere to YouTube's guidelines when using educational content on the platform.

Content that encourages harmful activities such as self-injury, drug use, or dangerous challenges may result in immediate penalties.

The portrayal of violent or graphic content, even in news or documentary contexts, should be handled cautiously to prevent glorification or sensationalization.

To prevent copyright strikes, refrain from re-uploading content that does not belong to you, particularly without appropriate attribution or authorization.

Fair use is a legally intricate doctrine that permits specific uses of copyrighted material. However, asserting the defense of "fair use" does not provide automatic immunity against copyright infringement claims. It is important to have a thorough understanding of the nuances.

When using music and audio, it is important to ensure that you are using royalty-free music or tracks that are licensed specifically to you. Copyright claims can arise from the use of popular songs, even in brief instances.

To achieve monetization, it is important to ensure that your content is suitable for advertisers. This entails refraining from using excessive profanity, discussing controversial subjects, or engaging in any form of content that may be considered inappropriate for a wide range of individuals.

Ensure that your titles, descriptions, and tags precisely reflect the content of your material. Misleading metadata can lead to demonetization or more severe consequences.

Child Safety and the Children's Online Privacy Protection Act (COPPA)

If your content targets children, it is important to consider compliance with COPPA regulations. Misclassification of content can result in substantial penalties.

Child exploitation, whether intentional or unintentional, will be subject to severe consequences.

To prevent spam and deceptive practices, it is important to follow certain guidelines.

Requesting subscribers in exchange for subscribing to other channels, commonly known as "sub4sub," is a violation of YouTube's guidelines.

Misleading thumbnails and titles, commonly known as clickbait, have the potential to generate higher click rates. However, if the level of deception becomes excessive, it may lead to policy violations.

Spamming comments, utilizing bots, or sharing links to malicious websites may result in receiving strikes.

Addressing Sensitive Topics: • Controversial Matters: When engaging in discussions about sensitive or controversial subjects, exercise caution and sensitivity. Contextualization and the avoidance of promoting detrimental conspiracies or misinformation are imperative.

When sharing news footage concerning wars, political conflicts, or other sensitive topics, it is important to provide context to prevent demonetization or strikes.

It is important to regularly review and update information.

Keep yourself informed. YouTube's policies are subject to change over time. It is advisable to regularly review guidelines and remain updated on any modifications.

Auditing previous content is necessary as changes in rules can render it problematic. It is important to regularly review older videos to ensure ongoing compliance.

In conclusion, effectively adhering to YouTube's policies entails more than simply avoiding prohibited content; it requires comprehending the platform's underlying principles. It is important to prioritize the creation of content that is genuine, authentic, and safe, while also respecting both the audience and the rules. By remaining knowledgeable and taking initiative, individuals can prioritize the creation of content that effectively connects with and captivates audiences, ultimately fostering a flourishing community.

CHAPTER 22

Engaging with Trends: Timely Content for a Boost in Views

Staying updated on current trends is crucial for YouTube creators aiming to enhance their viewership and expand their audience. Utilizing popular topics enables your content to capitalize on current interest, potentially catapulting your videos into the spotlight. This guide outlines strategies for effectively engaging with trends and producing timely content.

The Influence of Trending Topics:

Videos on trending topics attract a large number of views due to existing search queries and public interest.

YouTube's algorithm gives priority to content that resonates with users. Participating in popular trends can indicate to the algorithm that your video is pertinent and deserving of recommendation.

YouTube's Trending Page is a feature on the platform that

highlights popular and trending videos. A reliable resource for monitoring emerging trends. Always evaluate whether the topic is consistent with the theme of your channel.

Google Trends is a tool that provides information on the search popularity of terms over time. It can be used to gain insights into emerging and declining trends.

Social media platforms such as Twitter, TikTok, and Instagram can showcase popular subjects, challenges, or memes that could be suitable for adaptation on YouTube.

To authentically engage with trends, it is important to remain focused on your specific area of expertise or interest. The popularity of a certain trend does not necessarily indicate its suitability for incorporation into one's channel. Make sure that the topic is in line with your brand and target audience.

• Enhance the value: Avoid mere duplication. Evergreen vs. Trending Content: Comparing Long-lasting and Popular Topics

Achieving balance is crucial. Although trending content can provide temporary boosts, evergreen content, which refers to topics that remain relevant over time, offers long-term value. Achieve a harmonious equilibrium between the two opposing factors.

Certain trends have the tendency to evolve or resurface periodically. A contemporary interpretation of a past trend can still generate intrigue.

Timely Production: • Prompt Reaction: When a subject begins to gain traction, there is typically a limited timeframe to take advantage of its popularity. A streamlined production process facilitates timely publication of content on trending topics.

It is important to prioritize quality over speed. Low-quality content can have a detrimental impact on one's reputation, regardless of its relevance to current trends.

Engaging in viral challenges can enhance visibility, particularly when incorporating a unique twist or introducing novel elements.

Prioritize Safety: Take necessary precautions to ensure that the challenge adheres to YouTube's guidelines and does not pose any safety risks.

Collaboration on trends can enhance reach, particularly when creators explore a trending topic from different perspectives.

Cross-promotion involves sharing content related to a trend on various social platforms, which can help expand the reach of your content to a wider audience.

Analysis and Iteration: • Utilize YouTube Analytics to examine the performance of content published on a popular subject, and subsequently refine and improve based on the insights gained. Evaluate the effectiveness of past content and utilize this knowledge to inform future content decisions.

In conclusion, incorporating current trends is an effective strategy for maintaining the relevance of your content, attracting new viewers, and increasing the visibility of your channel. It is important to prioritize authenticity and avoid blindly following trends. Instead, choose trends that genuinely align with your content strategy. Effectively engaging with current topics can have a significant impact on growth and ensure the continued relevance of your YouTube channel within the dynamic YouTube environment.

CHAPTER 23

Behind the Scenes and Vlogs: Personalizing Your Channel

In the extensive realm of YouTube, establishing a personal connection serves as a crucial element in retaining viewers. Behind-the-scenes content and vlogs offer valuable insights into a creator's life and personality, serving as essential means to cultivate stronger connections with one's audience. Here is a guide on integrating these formats into your content strategy in an effective manner.

The Attraction of Authenticity:

Humanizing content refers to the process of making content more relatable and engaging for the audience by incorporating elements of human emotion, experiences, and storytelling. Polished videos demonstrate professionalism, whereas behind-the-scenes (BTS) footage and vlogs provide a glimpse into the individual behind the polished image, fostering relatability.

Trust Building: Authentic content facilitates trust and loyalty by bridging the gap between creators and viewers.

The Significance of Behind-the-Scenes Content in the Art Industry.

Preparation and Process: Provide insights into the research, scripting, or setup. This process clarification can enhance understanding and provide educational value to aspiring creators.

Bloopers and outtakes can be used to inject humor and demonstrate the human side of a person or production.

Please provide information about the equipment, setup, editing software, and any preferred tools that you use. This activity has the potential to be both informative and captivating.

Crafting Engaging Video Blogs:

Day in the Life: Illustrate a typical day or a noteworthy occasion. It provides viewers with a glimpse into your personal life beyond your regular content.

• Communicate Milestones: Engage your audience by sharing significant accomplishments, whether they pertain to the expansion of your channel or personal achievements, to involve them in your progress.

Sharing challenges and setbacks can enhance your approachability and provide viewers with valuable life lessons.

Maintaining Boundaries: • Emphasize Privacy: Despite the nature of vlogs and behind-the-scenes content, it is crucial to prioritize personal privacy and safety. It is advisable to refrain from disclosing personal information or specific locations that may pose a risk to your security.

• Emphasize Authenticity, Exercise Discretion: While it is important to be sincere, it is advisable to exercise caution in sharing every detail of your personal life. Establish your personal preferences.

Integrating with the main content is crucial.

Teasers: Utilize behind-the-scenes (BTS) footage as a means to generate anticipation for forthcoming primary content.

Complementary vlogs can enhance primary content themes, such as travel or cooking, by featuring relevant personal experiences or anecdotes.

Enhancing production value involves the use of engaging thumbnails and titles, which are essential for click-through rates, even in more casual content such as BTS and vlogs.

Storytelling is an essential aspect of vlogging, as it adds structure and purpose to the content, ensuring that it is not merely a collection of random footage. Develop an engaging narrative that captivates viewers throughout the entire duration.

Quality Control: It is important to maintain acceptable audio and video quality, even for casual content. It is advisable to consider investing in high-quality equipment such as a vlogging camera or microphone.

Engaging with one's audience is crucial.

Solicit prompt feedback from viewers regarding their preferences for future vlogs or behind-the-scenes (BTS) content, thereby promoting engagement and interaction.

Incorporate Q&A sessions into your vlogs to respond to inquiries or discuss comments from previous videos.

The importance of consistency and variety in various aspects.

• Consistent Schedule: To capitalize on the popularity of BTS and vlogs on your channel, it is advisable to incorporate them regularly, with a frequency of either weekly, bi-weekly, or monthly. • Diversify Content: It is recommended to introduce a variety of personal content to maintain audience interest. On certain occasions, the individual may choose to document the behind-the-scenes activities of a photoshoot, while on other occasions, they may opt to create a video blog showcasing a journey or event.

In conclusion, incorporating behind-the-scenes content and vlogs into your YouTube channel provides a genuine and intimate experience for viewers, fostering a stronger connection between them and the content creator. Although secondary content may have a more relaxed and spontaneous tone compared to primary content, incorporating some planning and storytelling can enhance its quality, transforming casual glimpses into engaging content. In the era of connectivity, personal and genuine moments tend to have the greatest impact.

CHAPTER 24

Next Steps: From YouTube Stardom to Wider Digital Domination

Achieving success as a prominent figure on YouTube is an immense accomplishment. In light of the ever-changing digital landscape, it is imperative for creators to expand their online presence and avoid dependence on a single platform. This chapter provides guidance on leveraging YouTube success and extending influence in the digital domain.

Utilizing Your YouTube Viewership:

Cross-promotion involves encouraging YouTube subscribers to follow the content creator on other platforms. This practice not only enhances your online visibility but also helps to maintain connectivity in the event of platform disruptions.

• Provide exclusive content across multiple platforms to

incentivize followers to engage with your brand across all channels.

Expanding into the Realm of Podcasting:

One option is to convert video content into podcasts or create a new audio series. Podcasts cater to individuals who desire content for their daily commutes, exercise routines, or leisure time.

Monetization opportunities for podcasts include sponsorships, ad placements, and paid subscriptions, similar to YouTube.

The popularity of short-form video content is increasing, with platforms such as TikTok, Instagram Reels, and Shorts gaining prominence. To engage with these audiences effectively, consider repurposing existing YouTube content or creating videos specifically tailored for each platform.

Consider exploring alternative live streaming platforms such as Twitch or Facebook Live if you have previously conducted live sessions on YouTube and your content is compatible with their user demographics.

Creating a Personal Website or Blog:

A website can serve as a centralized platform for storing various forms of content, including videos, articles, and merchandise.

Regular blog posts relevant to your content can enhance your search engine visibility and increase organic traffic, resulting in SEO benefits.

Merchandising and product strategies involve leveraging popularity to introduce a range of branded merchandise, including apparel and accessories.

Digital products such as e-books, courses, and exclusive

video content can be monetized, creating an additional source of revenue.

Engaging with Social Media

Maintain consistent branding across various platforms to facilitate easy recognition by fans.

Platform-specific strategies refer to the specific approaches or tactics that are tailored to a particular platform or technology. These strategies are designed to optimize performance and achieve specific goals on that platform. The content and engagement strategies employed on LinkedIn and Instagram will vary. Adapt your strategy according to the characteristics and preferences of the platform's user demographic and its unique advantages.

Collaborations and guest appearances are common practices in various artistic fields, such as music, film, and literature. These collaborations involve two or more individuals or groups coming together to create a joint work or to contribute to each other's projects. Guest appearances, on

To increase audience reach, it is advisable to engage in collaborations with influencers or brands on different platforms. This allows for the opportunity to access and connect with their existing audience.

Podcast guesting offers the opportunity to reach a wider audience and enhance one's credibility within a specific field.

Email marketing and newsletters offer a direct connection with subscribers, as emails are delivered directly to their inboxes without being subject to algorithms that control content visibility on other platforms.

Regular updates can be shared through weekly or monthly

newsletters, which offer a comprehensive summary of your content, updates, and exclusive insights.

Online workshops and webinars can be utilized to educate and engage participants, particularly if the host possesses expertise in a specific subject matter. This can effectively contribute to the establishment of authority in the given field.

Monetization opportunities can arise from premium workshops, which can serve as a means of generating income and enhancing one's digital portfolio.

It is important to remain informed and adapt to changes.

The digital landscape is constantly evolving. Stay updated on current trends, platforms, and tools.

Continuous learning involves dedicating time to acquiring new skills, such as mastering new editing tools, understanding platform algorithm intricacies, and developing digital marketing strategies.

In conclusion, achieving fame on YouTube marks the initial stage of one's digital trajectory. To establish yourself as a prominent digital influencer, it is crucial to diversify your online presence and adapt to the ever-changing digital landscape. This will help solidify your position beyond being solely recognized as a YouTube personality. This involves utilizing your strengths, exploring new opportunities, and consistently providing value to an expanding audience.